AF084008

29°

Sunny

today

First edition, 2024
Copyright © Leonardo Dardy
www.leonardodardy.com
@leonardo_dardy

All rights reserved. Apart from any fair dealing for private study, research, criticism or review permitted under the Copyright Act 1968, no part of this book may be reproduced, stored, copied, translated or used in any manner without written permission of the copyright owner. Enquiries should be made to the copyright owner.

ISBN: 978-0-646-89291-7

In collaboration with Back Shed Press (Melbourne)

Cover and illustrations by Marie Zubatá

Back cover photograph by Connor Bishop

Content

11 let's do everything in the world
13 have a good day
15 diving
16 just a comforting fact
18 a poem
22 Jean-Paul Belmondo
25 anniversary
27 one day you might meet someone
28 an honest blunt girl
32 an old soul
34 get them
35 an overheard discussion from the next door
37 she just didn't speak, man
40 a post on Byron Bay Rental Sleuth
41 over it
43 29° sunny today
46 a random facebook status
52 these pubs
54 you look like Johnny Depp
56 Jane
58 A r g e n t i n a !
60 Murakami
62 I met a so-called artist today
64 the best wedding
65 a poem written when drunk
66 there are funnier stories in this world
70 shit and fart jokes
72 tinder blues
74 a handsome motherfucking man, Leonardo Dardy
76 seš moc hezká
77 crispy chicken

79 a bloody accountant
81 cancel Byron Baes
84 a fat guy
86 I like vegans, gays, and punks
88 a real man
90 1%
94 the sun also rises
96 instagram blues á la Byron Bay
100 every day I do this
104 cancer
106 thanks, Cavanbah
108 1 minute silence
110 happy for now
114 here it comes again

29° sunny today leonardo dardy

let's do everything in the world

she rocked up
excited
like
a maniac

let's do this let's do that
and
let's do this other thing
too –

in 3 seconds she managed to say
all the words in the world

and I

got tired –

jesus christ, she said, *why are you yawning*

you

need to get a life –

*you need to
dance*

*you need to
do yoga*

(I've done some)

*you need to
start a ceramic course*

*you need to
see the waterfalls around and try
surfing and why aren't you outside
it's so sunny –*

oh boy

I got

so tired

I

fell asleep

have a good day

8 o'clock in the morning –

a man hula hooping
on the street
wearing a rainbow tee
making
everyone's day –

joy
he's singing
waving all around
and love
only
love –

I'm walking right his way
and when I notice him
I cross the street
to the opposite pavement –

too much energy can be a very uncomfortable
and awkward thing;

I don't know how to react to it –

but that guy
probably about 60? –
man
didn't he look like
really
believing
in
a good day –

and I crossed, now I owe him —
so I thought I'd borrow his message
and pass it on
though
a quieter way —

have a good day

diving

there was some blues playing
not the best blues
but blues it was – and then
the first singer was replaced by another
and that's when it got even worse –

badness is a place
I'm not pleased to be
but it's an effort, too –
and hard-working effort
is allowed – it's better than shining
from an undeserved pedestal –

badness is a form of self-pity –
loss of perspective
and ability to discern – cliché
and lies –
sometimes too much soul
or
selling a soul – but badness
is also
a good fight –

that's why I'm going home
to dive into my bad night
bad
but dignified night –
perhaps sad
perhaps the saddest night –
but
dignified
night

just a comforting fact

there's no one to trust
never was, and
never will be — even me
I can't trust myself

why would I — you say
you'd never do this, then
I see you doing it — I say
I'd never do that, then
you see me doing it —

loyalty, what a lie
hidden inside a nice value —
I'm okay with it
I take it
as a necessity —

to see you coming home
high as hell — blaming yourself
for the filthy night
you are now trying to
wash away
from your body
by taking
an endless shower —

I have, too, come home
that way
many times — feeling like
killing myself — by the unbelievable
amount of bullshit
I've done —

we can't blame each other — but nobody
can trust anybody — that
is a fact — spiritually balanced —
just a comforting fact based on

transience

a poem

it's always been
about a poem

and always will be
about a poem

but more it's about
life, you say –

life's not poetry, you say
but it has its moments – when
pain
offers romance – turns grey
into blue –

or out of nowhere – as always
somehow – for
a second, or
two – a smile – perhaps
even
a whole laugh –

that's what I call
a poem, you say – what
a life –

a poem – but more it's
about you
trying to get up
from your knees
and re-set that
fucking smile
back over your face –

if you've been there, you know
what I mean: there's
no poetry
at all —

and that's what makes it a poem

Jean-Paul Belmondo

I remember I would
borrow
my mum's bra
and put it
on my knees

just to learn how to unhook it —

I would sniff it, too
for some reason — as it
somehow
turned me on —

but

mostly

I was just training —

I did it

thousands of times; without looking

chewing gum

trying to look like

Antonio Banderas

or Jean-Paul Belmondo —

I'd also borrow a ciggy
from my mum's drawer
and suck on it unlit

just to look sexier
because
I knew
or I at least
hoped
that one day —
one day
my time
would come —

and then
all of a sudden
my time
really
had
come —

I
Leonardo Dardy
was in bed
with a girl
for the first time
in my life — and I
I shone — I really
sold
what I had learnt —

oh god —
how skilfully
I unhooked it —
to this day
I can see
the spark
in her eyes —

I was

like a god

for a second —

I was

Jean-Paul Belmondo

anniversary

the other day I happened – to think –
of you –
what for Christ's sake was it
that I used to love so much –

while thinking hard
I kept finding
only massive amounts
of idiotic toxicity, cheap emotions
and the other
fun things –

right now looking at my girlfriend
calmly arguing with someone
in the corner
of this pub – if the falseness of a judgment
is an objection to a judgment
or not – I can see that skill of hers – to stay open
to confrontations –

and there, as a bonus, that willingness
to piss in the sink

for a laugh:

I should be a happy man –

and you somewhere
on the other side of the world
you still think something –
about truth, about victory
something
about relationships

and your friends confirm everything for you —

man, what was it that I used to love so much
and *still* somehow do — I think to myself —
remembering the good times
when I didn't see what I can see now —

then I light up my ciggy — take a drag —
I nod at the sky
as some sort of a thanks
and hope-you're-doing-great —

then I take
another drag
and forget about you
for another year

one day you might meet someone

one day you might meet someone
who would – bury – you
in compliments
but at the same time you may find out –
how good

honesty

must be – cruel;

that's how it moves one –

I am wild
and lazy
and useless –
sometimes I win
and sometimes
I lose –

but the core is clear
nothing's a competition –

you don't have to be
tough
but ready
instead

if you want to know
how to laugh
when
under fire

an honest blunt girl

I met a girl today, an honest
blunt one

without all the bullshit around —

she seemed to know
some happiness
as well as
some pain

so the conversation was quite okay —

she didn't seem to judge
anything
as she knew what it feels like
to be judged

but

was still able to judge for the sake of humour

and quality —

she was my kind of woman, not afraid
to reveal basics —
like how many people she's slept with, or
who's had
the biggest and hairiest balls —

she didn't seem to romanticise
anything
but was able to make romance out of
everything —

my kind of woman, like I said —

expects nothing from life

but what it is —

then all made sense when she told me

she was a stripper —

someone who may well understand life
but will never be heard properly —

that's when I knew she had me

and I happily gave in

an old soul

you see me in my bed
sleeping till 12pm
every day – you think –
oh my god
he really does sleep
a lot – when
is he going to wake up? –

it's 1pm and you're sure
I must be reading a book
or something – you check on me –
and there he is
still
sleeping –

there is a lawn mower in full stride
in the neighbour's backyard – there are
builders working on a new fence –
banging out
the old planks – Paul next door turned on
a bloody chainsaw
to cut the tree –

and he
is
still sleeping – there are mates
going to the pub – some taking their cars
going on trips –

around Australia – exciting – but hey he's
still sleeping –

then it's 3pm, 29° sunny
and you gave up –
you craved company, sun
drinks;
I'm waking up, having no purpose – feeling
grey – thinking:

an old soul?
therefore a tired soul –
excited by the tiredness
though

get them

everybody got a warning letter –
there are going to be these fence guys
behind your house –
they'll be working on a new fence –

it's going to happen from Monday to Wednesday
8am-12pm – it may affect your sleep –

then Monday rocked up and
there they were on time, the fence guys
working
on a new fence –

that's when my neighbour stormed out
from her house –

"guys," she shouted, "I'm tired. can you be quiet, please?

it's 8am, cunts –

eight fucking A.M. you fucking cunts!"

an overheard discussion from the next door

T: my mum calls me Terry
T2: OH MY GOD THATS REALLY COOL MY MOM CALLS ME TERRY TOO
T: NO WAY DOES SHE DO YOU MEAN IT???
T2: YEAH OH MY GOD I JUST MET YOU BUT I LOVE YOU SO MUCH ALREADY
E: OH MY GOD I KNEW THEY WERE GONNA LOVE EACH OTHER
Jolene: my boyfriend calls me Joe and I always PUNCH him for it I HATE IT SO MUCH
T: OH NOOOO REALLY
T2: HAHAHAHAHAHAHAHAHAHAHAHAHAHAHA
E: NO WAY I CANT BELIEVE IT
T: I'M SORRY TO INTERRUPT but I'M SO EXCITED TO TELL YOU I bought a handbag yesterday and I'm SURE you'll LOVE IT
E: Oh Did you
T2: Oh Did you SHUT UP ARE YOU JOKING THIS GONNNNNA SOUND AS IF I WAS MAKING IT UP BUT guess what ME TOO I TOO BOUGHT A HANDBAG RECENTLY WE ARE TWINS!!!
T: WE ARE TWINS!!!
V: OH MY GOD THEY ARE TWINS
E: HAHAHAHAHAHAHAHAAHAHAHAHAHAHAHAHAHAHAHAHAHAHAHAHAHAHAHAHAHAHAHAHAHAHAHAHAHAHAHAHAHAHA HAHAHAHAHAHA THATS SO FUNNY I LOVE YOU GIRLS
T: HAHAHA LOOK at it though it's BEAUTYYY

T2: Look at mine – What do YOU THINK?
E: Oh is it crocodile leather??
T2: YEAH it's SOOOO beautiful isn't it??
T: It is VERY beautiful, how much was it?
T2: 2500 bucks but this one is still cheap when comparing to other ones there
T: Oh that's pretty good
Jolene: I love both of them girls. Oh I feel so nice today isn't it a beautiful day???
T: yeah right?? me toooo and the whole night is about to CooOOOoOOOo-OOOme
T2: PARTYYYY
E: HOOORAYYYYYYYYY
V: PAAARTYYYYY HOOORAYYYY HAHAHAHAHA-HAHAHAHAH
Jolene: HAHAHAHAHAAAAAAAAAAAAAAAAAAAA HAHAHAHAHAHAHA

she just didn't speak, man

she just
didn't speak
man –
there were people
living with us – moving
in
and out
almost every month –

and they would be trying
to talk
to her – so the awkward silence
had a chance
to be filled
with some
welcoming atmosphere –

but she
man
she only
ANSWERED
questions
she never
ASKED back –

after 10 minutes of silence
in the kitchen
they would ask her
"did you work today?"
and she'd answer
"no,
I did not" –

oh, man
and I'm in my room, right —
laughing — it's painful
though
to hear all those people
trying to talk to her —
trying to get to know
their housemate
trying to find something
in common —
"do you like cooking?"
"no,
I do not" —

then she opens the door
of my room —
"damn it," she says, "what
am I supposed to do?!" —
"I don't know," I say, "but
at least
expand your sentences
ask something back — otherwise
it's so
fucking
awkward
man" —

"why am I always
FORCED
to talk to people! I don't
know
HOW
to do it! I'm not even
interested in them!" —

then after a few hours
she's hungry again —
she makes sure
nobody's in the kitchen
she goes in there
and while taking food
from the fridge
there he is
yay
another housemate coming —

"oh hey, hon, how are you today?"
"good," she says
"oh, that's good"
"you?"
"yeah, good hon, thanks"
"nice" —

fucking hell, I think to myself

a post on Byron Bay Rental Sleuth

"Hello,

I'm 29 years old girl looking for a new place to call home.

I love yoga, meditation, the beach, outdoors and surfing.

I don't drink or party, smoke
and like to start my day early,
watching the sunrise. I'm never home.

I'm clean, easy going and respectful of other peoples privacy.

Every answer will be much appreciated,

yours sincerely
Nicolette"

over it

I'm watching some
disgusting porn
oh, man
and it's so fantastically kinky
that
you have to
you just
have to –

there's something
so over the edge
so stupid
so horny
so depraved
so perverse
and shameful
that you just have to
jerk off over shemale
bukkake
creampie

over double penetration
over fetish
over old/young
over bondage
over cartoon
over it
over midgets
over glory holes
animals
and faeces

and all that

all that

you'll try to forget about
as soon as you're done –

but man

you have to

you just

have to

29° sunny today

29° and sunny today —
another day
to stay home
with the blinds drawn
so the sun doesn't have to
argue with me;

that's the problem with the sun —
it tempts great men to go out
to go to the beach
to laugh with all those sunny people —
it tempts with such determination
that even great men
forget to observe the darkness of their room;

29° and sunny today —
and I don't even have one reason
why I should be out there —
except that I secretly like the feeling
of
being tanned

a random facebook status

Leekey Nicole
My hopes for a good job have been dashed again, the reason why they chose someone else is humiliating, she's younger and therefore more "useful" than me ...this is what my colleague heard and texted me ... I'm sorry, it's simply fucked up, I really don't know what else to do ...

We all will be older one day, does anyone get that? So what about me, if I'm useless, should I hang myself or find some bullshit work somewhere in a factory? What is better? God, I'm sick again............

10 h

> **George Flynn**
> Keep your head up, Nicole. There's plenty of work everywhere.
> 9 h
>
> **Leekey Nicole**
> yeah, for instance...? with my equipment..my age, my handicap..
> 8 h · Edited

Catherine Nes
Nic, I'm sorry for you. With your experience and language skills.. You can always find some shitty job somewhere, but to get a good, dignified one is a skill nowadays. At Brooze & Sons they offered me pretty good money
8 h · Edited

David Walls
Fingers crossed you find something soon ?
8 h

Leekey Nicole
David Walls I'm so desperate that I'll do /except a whore/ anything ...... but even that "anything" ... they are not interested... I really don't know what to do anymore
8 h

Mary Mair
I know that feeling very well...that helplessness, anger... Here for you, Nic
7 h

Leo McClurry

Try some hotels in the mountains. There's a shortage of staff. They're offering accommodation and food for free. They finally accept doggies too. you know the language. If you could do half a year you could put yourself together. it's not ideal but what is...don't hang yourself you silly goose. Fingers crossed, love you Nic.

6 h

Leekey Nicole

Leo McClurry I've been thinking about it but I don't know who to approach..I'm good at caregiving, my clients liked me, but physically I just can't be on my legs so many hours anymore .. I feel .. I feel trapped.. trapped.... I don't know what to do. what to do??? what's the soluion....pure.........desperation...

7 h

Leo McClurry

Leekey Nicole reach out everybody just to increase your chances.. but they're looking everywhere...no need for desperation.. where else will you get a good money like that? I've got ome contacts for you.

1 h

Alex Colonel
Well you can do some bullshit job for a while while looking for something better at the same time
7 h · Edited

Leekey Ivana
Alex Colonel I guess that's how it is going to turn out in the end.....
7 h

Heidi Diamant
Alex Colonel life dream...behind the cash desk..fuck it all..
19 m

Michaela Brooks
ever thought about moving to the country? I'm also looking for a job and looks like there are socialworkers needed (not only mobile care, but just counselling etc.) They will arrange and reimburse you or t ... **See more**
30 m

these pubs

that pub
is emptier
and emptier – even me –
I don't want to go there
anymore –

but somehow I still happen
to be there
every night – talking bullshit – getting naked –
postponing all the potential potentials –

don't get me wrong – potentials are something
to laugh at – in this ambitious society – but
they got you trapped too, my man – even though
every potential has grown in a pub – and
every potential needs a beer to cool down –

you think it'd be nice
to have time – to realize – and when
you're finally standing up to run away
there he is again – the bartender –
coming with another round of pints –
"on the house,"
he says, "for my bezzies" –

man, if I was
a real man, I would get up
and say, "no, man,
I'm going home
to read" – and he'd be
amazed
by me –

but for some reason I just happen
to be sitting there
drinking that thing
until closing time – then
looking for another pub –

these pubs
are emptier and emptier – even me –
I don't wanna be there
anymore –
but somehow I still happen
to be here
every night

you look like Johnny Depp

"I give myself to you / as long as we move / on the floor" Idles

two women at a bar —
a mother
with her daughter
looking at me
curiously —

I finish
my drink
and I get
closer

"hey, ladies," I say, "what's going on?" —

they are looking at me
speechless, surprised
impressed —
they're studying
every detail of what I wear
everything
I do —

"you remind us of someone," the mother says
"who might that be?" I humour them
"some actor," the daughter joins
"James Franco?"
"no, yeah, but…"
"is it perhaps James Byron Dean the man?"
"no… nah, not really…"
"jesus christ, man," cries the daughter out triumphantly, "you look like Johnny Depp!"

"that's the one!" the mother hugs her daughter
"well, ladies, then it looks like the time has come
for Johnny to get us three a drink"
"yes, Johnny! please!"
"don't you worry, mum," I say

and get us drinks right away –

"I give myself to you," I tell them, "as long as
we move on the floor!"

and in a second
we are

dancers, hip to hip –
dancing, cheek to cheek –

kissing

in a grand Johnny Depp style

Jane

I fell in love with you – like I
probably would have
with anybody else – in the
right place
at the right time – but now
it's all yours –

you disappeared in the drunk night –
when all I could do
was scream nonsense
and whip my willy out – for the girls
thems
& the boys
to admire – not realising that
I should ask you
for more than
just your first name –

that I might have disgusted
your possible interest
I take as a proof
we're not meant for each other –
but what frustrates me
is that somewhere

between the willy
and the screaming – I, the idiot, was
quite very possibly
really falling in love with you –

and now I can't find you – I googled – I went through
the whole
facebook event –
I thought hard – nothing –

there are only a few
fleeting moments
of your blue? eyes
and likely a wrong first name –

well, Jane, what happens now? –
let's just hope
I'll ask more questions
next time

Argentina!

last night, I was from
Argentina – my first language
was Spanish
and I
loved football – and

that guy

called Messi – and
all the other
beloved players
of our country –

last night, we absolutely destroyed
France – and once we did that, I
stormed out from the bar
and hugged
every living soul
on this planet –

A – r – g – e – n – t – i – n – a – !
A – R – G –
E – N –
T – I – N – A – ! –

my country confirmed
we were
the best in the world
once again –
and I
of course
couldn't be more
proud –

I happily accepted
all those
free trippple whiskeys
for the bartender's fellow Argentinians
and kept pretending
I
cared – on this historical day
of football –
19th of December 2022

Murakami

I've noticed
Murakami's books
on the shelf
at this house party –

and the guy
who lived there
just happened to be
next to me
at that moment –

"Murakami's shit, man," I told him, "why
have you got
his terrible books
on your shelf?" –

he asked me why he was shit –

"he's just shit," I said
with drunk and broken
English, "and the fact you've got him
on your shelf
suggests
you're shit too!" –

that guy, he got angry
and started screaming at me
so much
it got the attention
of all the people around –
he
completely destroyed me
with entirely valid arguments –

and then – he
kicked me out –
and I
walked home
knowing
I've never read
Murakami –

but I've read that guy's poetry –
too proud
to take a joke
has never led
to any good writing

and then I stopped
and looked him
right
in his eyes –

"well," I said, "that's part of the fun though, no?"

"no," he said, "I would

rather

forget

about her" –

that's when I realised
he wasn't only a coward –
but mainly
a fake
artist

I met a so-called artist today

I met a so-called artist today

he said

"my girlfriend just broke up with me" –

so I started laughing – I
started clapping
my hands –
I jumped up
as high as
I could – I started yelling –

"look at that poor guy
his girlfriend
just broke up
with him!

he sure wasn't
enough for her!
she sure thinks
he's a loser!

look at that poor guy!" –

I was jumping around
like a monkey
screaming
hooray
hooray
let's celebrate
let's
celebrate

the best wedding

there was this wedding
that M & D went to —

they called it the best
as everything was
just as planned —

the setting beautifully done & the catering
everybody in a good mood & families got together

&

everything simply magical —

but then M asked D to go with her to the toilet
and when opening the wrong door

they saw the groom having sex
with one of the waitresses —

they closed the door
and went on enjoying the night;

when dancing, M just whispered to D
she was grateful for their relationship
and kissed him —

they never told anybody

and the wedding remained forever the best

a poem written when drunk

there are funnier stories in this world

it's just a bit
funny
to watch your father disappear
but
that guy, you don't really care about
it's been
20 years now —

when it's your sister though —
drowning in booze
talking horseshit
she can't even pronounce properly anymore —
two chins
pale reddish puffy face
dead eyes — it's a bit
so to speak
funnier — to see all the potential, all

the beauty your mates dreamed to conquer

dying

despite your mother's desperate weeps —

it's just a bit
funny — the blind
and deaf
tears
of someone
who gives up
everything
for another
sip —

it's

just a bit

funny —

but I know there are
perhaps
funnier stories
in this world —

perhaps the one
of comparing pains
that doesn't
really work

shit and fart jokes

the more she suffered
the more she laughed —
my mother seemed to be
just like that —

she could laugh all day
and even though she loved
shit and fart jokes; dumb
jokes —

she would give you
the genuine feeling
that whatever humour
you've got
you're
loved —

even if you had none
she would see it
as one — she would
just laugh —

despite living on the street
with her 3 kids
after running away
from a man
who was beating her up
on and off
for
20 years

she was laughing — she
couldn't buy us anything —

she would, though, allow us
to say some naughty words

for a laugh –

the more she suffered
the more she seemed she wanted
to see
the whole world
laughing –

and when I had a bit of a bad day lately
I accidentally laughed –

my mum suddenly appeared from up above:

"that's the way," she said, "keep laughing,

son"

tinder blues

study nursing, love to travel and will 100percent beat you in a cod 1v1 and I have a gorgeous doggo :P
— Jane, 22, 25 kilometres away

Someone get my attention, Im bored. If your COVID vaccinated you are an idiot, swipe left. ;)
— Gena.pena, 29, 93 kilometres away

i dont mean to brag but i have a really chokeable throat
— Perazia, 23, 62 kilometres away

Just ask way. no expectations = no disappointment
— Elizabeth, 44, 19 kilometres away

I dont like tinder :)

I like music
— Maia, 25, 11 kilometres away

I'm not into party boys, smokers, drinkers or coward. I'm not here for anything sexual, just looking for diner buddy at first and and possibly more later. (I love meat so Vegan swipe left
— Ezry, 28, 44 kilometres away

just moved to the Goldcoast, here to meet people, I'm the kinda gal who will eat the last piece of your garlic bread
— Ev, 22, 32 kilometres away

ready to get back in the game
— **Lea, 68, 3 kilometres away**

I'm Japanese <3
a great obstacle to happiness is to expect too much happiness
— **Dina, 29, 84 kilometres away**

It's guaranteed that we will not get along if you listen to Ed sheeran
— **Aisha 19, 2293 kilometres away**

pleast) Please don't fucking wasted my time if you not gonna meet, I'm not a optimistic person. I don't need folowers because I don't have instagram, Snapchat or WhatsApp.
— **Xena, 32, 112 kilometres away**

I honestly dunno what I am doing here hahahahaha but I published my frist poetry book
— **Nicky 22, 15 kilometres away**

I'm Argentinian Student. Biologist :P:P
— **Chle, 25, 23 kilometres away**

a handsome motherfucking man, Leonardo Dardy

so I met a girl, right
another one —

a nice damn bloody girl, gorgeous one
one that I could easily fall in love with —

but she

didn't want me

can you believe it? —

I, of course, kept telling her, *man, I am
Leonardo Dardy
you should want me*

but

she

she just didn't —

there must be something wrong, I said
*look at me
carefully
from all sides
you
really
do not see it?*

*a handsome motherfucking man
Leonardo Dardy —*

but she

surprisingly

she really just didn't –

*the people you want, they
don't want you*, I thought

and noticed my last chance
to save the night –

as always, I woke up in the morning
with someone –
who I wasn't born for
and who wasn't born
for me

seš moc hezká

jednou ty tvý žhavý oči
zmizí v jiných

s tim počítám –

případná bolest je i bránou ke klidu
když skrz ní prostoupíš moudře
můžeš poznat
že člověk je na světě
především sám
až pak ve společnosti;

takový vědění je důstojný
má kuráž, odhodlání
humor
i styl –

a koneckonců
je spousta válek na to
abych se staral
o tyhle malý –

ale to si piš, snažit se o tebe budu
seš moc hezká

crispy chicken

yes, sure I see them
swinging under your shirt
every time you're going
to run food –

and yes, I see those tattoos
those piercings and all
the greater signs
that I could love you so much
I'd forget how I love my girlfriend –

and here we are then, I am frying
this crispy chicken
and soon you will run it –
I'll say, "crispy chicken, table 27, please"
you'll look me right in the eyes
and say
"yes
chef" –
then you'll go your way
and I'll go mine –

fuck, and yes
no –
maybe I shouldn't send
any crispy chicken
anymore –
because
usually
attraction
lessens
when

too close
to reality —

it's very probable then
that if we got too close
to reality
there would be nothing left —

but my girlfriend
running all the crispy chicken

a bloody accountant

there was a new guy on a trial
in the kitchen –

I didn't tell the big dogs
but, well, that guy, he
didn't even seem to be able
to fill up a piping bag
with cream –

and when he did
the cream
was everywhere – it was
on his apron, on his
two tea towels – he even had it
in his bloody hair –

and he kept asking, what should he do
with it – I told him, man, no worries, probably
just clean it – then he did, and had a lot more
questions for me – I got nervous as well
because
I don't know how to tell people what to do –

jesus christ, wasn't I even more nervous
than him – suddenly, I screwed up my job
too – the big dogs saw it and asked
what I was doing –

"I'm just stupid," I said
guessing
that certain anxieties
can't be properly
understood –

another colleague was behind me now

he said

"that new guy
he looks like a bloody accountant –

doesn't he?"

cancel Byron Baes

I got this job
as a dishie
and soon became
the best
and most famous
dishwasher
in Australia –

so now when I teach new dishwashers
how to dishwash – I immediately notice
their lack of wisdom
in their movement
with plates
pots
and cutlery –

they don't dance
they don't know the tricks
they don't get along with the sink –
but most importantly
they don't know
that everything you do
should be done with some style
some kind of
dignity, some
grace – yes, you might be
without motivation
but you still want to wash
that beautiful plate
of yours
like nobody
before you –

yeah, that's right — one so slow
it just drives you crazy — the second one
slow, no ideas, and rude at the same time —
rude, that's okay — if you know
how to dance though — the third one
hey, pretty fast, but speaking all the time —
about bullshit — going for ciggies —
ciggies, that's okay — bullshit is not —
a good dishwasher doesn't speak
about techno —
but Dostoevsky
or
Tolstoy, or even
Shelley
would be OK —

so the last time I supervised a new dishwasher
I told him
man
please
don't make your colleagues sad
play it fair
offer some help, man — be thoughtful, man
don't make other people's lives hard —
they see you
even though most of them
are too kind to say the truth out loud
they see you, man
they see
how unfair you are
how you don't think
of others
how you don't give a damn
about dishwashing —

something
so
beautiful – so
noble –
so
essential – they see
what a shit show
you perform
what
a bloody
shit
show
you perform

a fat guy

every morning there was
a pretty fat guy – like
a really
fat guy – running – sweating
his ass off
every morning –

every morning – for
2 months – I would sit
on the beach
reading – secretly
watching him – and one day

I got up –

"listen," I said, "you know you're doing
a great fucking job, right?" –

he smiled as if
nobody had ever told him – as if
people
didn't tell anything nice to each other
anymore –

"thank," he stuttered, "thank you,"

and then

he ran even faster

I like vegans, gays, and punks

I like
gentle people
perhaps because
I was raised
in the absence
of my father –

I like vegans, gays
and punks –
perhaps because they seem
to understand
how – it feels like –
to be left out –

and anytime I see
someone manly
I sense rivalry
as if they were my absent father –
too late
to give me a lesson
in how to be a man –

I don't really know
how to chop wood
or fight
but my anger gets me
through every
violent situation –

my father seems to have left
a pretty unprepared son
behind –

but by having done that
he paradoxically created
a fun
playground
under my feet —

I seem to know women
more than men
perhaps because
I was raised
by my mother —
and safety I feel
only
late at night
when falling asleep
with a woman
I love —

I am a man — who
hides his own weaknesses
in sarcasm, irony
and scepticism — and who
appreciates those
who listen
ask
and know
how — it feels like —
to be left out

a real man

there was a deep voice speaking
behind the fence
in my neighbour's backyard
so deep
I had to get up
and see
what the man looked like —

through a little gap
between two planks of wood
I first caught
a glimpse of his toes —
then I moved to the next gap
and slowly continued
to his knees
and thighs —

they weren't male legs
at all — no — not
at all —
they looked feminine
they looked
like female legs — very
long and skinny
but
hairy —

I was impressed —
then the voice was back on it
speaking —
I was
shocked — I —

I didn't know
what to do – *should I
run away?* –

I couldn't
run away – I was
trapped
in curiosity – I mean
what a voice – what a deep
goddamn
voice – I was
slowly making my way
towards his face – *what
does he look like?* –

then I finally got there – guess
what – it was
really
a man – a real
man –
with a deep voice
and long long
skinny
fantastically feminine
legs

1%

it's quite simple — the best workers
come from the worst jobs, just like
the best musicians
from the worst times —

if you're one of them, you know
99% of music sucks — same for
all the other arts, every other
human being —

and the
1%
you'll never hear
as the best hide
in the corner
of their room
wanting to be
uninvolved —

while you think
you're
so special
they
keep working
the dish pit
trying to
wash
the plate
of theirs
the best
they
can —

and then they go home
through the darkness of their city
enjoying
the 1% —

while the 99% already fell asleep
in the fresh sheets that have never been dirty —

always so far from reality — always
feeling like winners — always
wrongly famous

the sun also rises

another summer
is gone – and I
didn't even notice
it was here – that I
could've gone
to a park –

or drank a bottle of wine
at night
sitting in the city
next to a river – I could have had a moment;
summer breeze blowing
through my hair –

drunk, I would go to a bar then –
meet someone, have
fun – then go home – hand
in hand
with a nice girl – make breakfast
in the morning –

yet another summer
just passed by – and I
didn't go
on a road trip – for
a swim – I didn't even
buy myself
an ice cream –

the whole summer I spent
in my room – on my phone –
jerking off – swiping on dating apps –

reading war news
& celebrity gossip –

only once did the sun rise –
when Brett and I
were driving to the beach to camp there –
licking an ice cream
sipping on wine –

I stuck my head out of the window
John Prine's *In Spite of Ourselves*
on the radio –
all these goosebumps and butterflies and

Jesus Christ

keep your sunny days –
but know
at times
I loved them
too

instagram blues á la Byron Bay

strongwoman344 Even though this year I met the most broken version of me I also met the strongest version of me

> **wow5** 6h
> oh I love that so much
> **Reply**

nobigdeal Deeping my devotion to the waters, honouring the ancient connection I feel to the spirit of water. Excited to see how this continues to open and expand my life. So much medicine in listening and submerging in the waters of the earth.

> **jozeedone** 8h
> I love reading your wisdom. Thank you for sharing
> **Reply**   **See Translation**

matthewneverdies Music islike heart Like fire is soul

> **beebeezeebeautifulhuman** 4h
> oh mate a stunning verse that
> **Reply**
>
>> **matthewneverdies** 3h
>> @beebeezeebeautifulhuman thanks bro bro i've spent hours thinking how to express this...
>> **Reply**

ohmankissmyash I am grateful for every heartbeat that has brought me to here. For my healthy body. For my friends. For my strength to follow my dreams. For water. I want to acknowledge all the people that I am grateful and hold so much love for. You see my talents and push me towards the better version of me. I wouldn't be able to do all the things I do without you. You mean the world to me.

> **thatsright8** 6h
> so much love for you xx
> **Reply**

> **ifeelsoalienatedhere** 5h
> oh that made me cry Ash.. so well expressed
> **Reply**

> **imissczechrepublic** 3h
> I can't believe we met only a year ago. It feels like 30 years. I love you so much for being in my life and for you being so you. Endless love for you. You're such a talented and beautiful human being. You truly are.
> **Reply**
>
>> **ohmankissmyash** 1h
>> **@imissczechrepublic** oh dear Lena, you know I feel the same way about you. thanks for being vulnerable.
>> **Reply**

epipipi.fart.i.am.stinky.ry sometimes we get so caught up in our heads we forget about this kind of stuff thats actually going on in the world. Are you spending your days and your time worrying about things that have happened in your past or you're just letting them go. Are you spending your time and days worrying about whats happening in the future, or you enjoying your time today. I'm moving in a couple of days, im living by myself because my housemates are already gone, it doesnt worry me, I am not stressed, I am excited, I cant fucking wait, wherever I land I land, you know, no expectations, no disappointment, go and enjoy yourself, go and enjoy your friends, go and hug somebody, go hug a tree, go and do something fucking fun today. If you can't because you gotta go to work today tell them that you ate curry last night and go and shit yourself go home, fuck that. It's monday. Do not go to work for somebody else. You are powerful. Fuck the system. Whats your body telling you to do. Is it to go for a run? Is it to go and plant a flower? Money will come money will go. Your life is short, not long. We are only a little blitz in this fucking universe. Go and live your life. re you doing it???

> **john349_bobo** 8h
> ok I don't go to work but now I don't have how to pay the rent
> **Reply**
>
> > **epipipi.fart.i.am.stinky.ry** 5h
> > @john349_bobo honeyyou're

powerful. Believe in yourself.
Go enjoy your life.
Screw the system
Reply

youradviceisgood4 5h
100% Rachel. Monday is not a day to work. And exactly...we're just a little blitz in this massive universe...
Reply

itsall5wise 3h
I adore you, and am so proud of your growth. What a blessing it is to walk these days together. My heart honours the heart in you
Reply

imsoenligthtenedicantbelieveit55 2h
I'm seeing myself from a new perspective today, just because of you, seeing a power in myself I never quite believed in. How I've longed for this for so long..
Reply

leonardo_dardy 1h
wow amazing
Reply

every day I do this

they got me — I
do yoga now — I'm one of them
now — I
box
and I
run every day and go for a swim
every day — I

meditate and listen to podcasts
about higher living — I
sit in the sun! — I
am vegan now — I woke up early
and made myself a Buddha bowl
today
with a freshly squeezed
OJ — I
sit in the sun! —

I sit in the sun — I feel great, and I
talk with people, and
don't drink anymore, I
don't drink anymore, or smoke, I
don't smoke
anymore —

and I repeat to myself
that beautiful quote
Jamie
always says – *"follow
your dreams"* – oh
Jamie
how beautiful –

I exercise – every day – and read
self-help books
every day
and
I dance – and I
do yoga
every day – and go for a swim
these days
every day – every day
I fucking do this
every day – every
single
motherfucking
day
I do this

cancer

this woman, man —
she
survived cancer — 3
times — and she
always
had this
huge smile
on her face —

I never understood
that smile —
that smile
really annoyed me — she smiled
so much
there were almost tears
in her eyes —

"stop fucking smiling
all the time," I always thought —

it was only recently
that I found myself
feeling healthy
after a long period
of illness

and I

happened
to have
a similar smile
to hers —

I think

I

finally

seemed

to understand

gratitude

thanks, Cavanbah

thanks, Byron Bay — I mean
Cavanbah — for all the girls
you've brought into my life — the English
they've taught me — the hangovers
I've travelled more than
your nature —

thanks for all the trips I've
never done — thanks to Mt. Warning
I've never climbed — all the waterfalls
I've never seen — surfing — I've never
tried — for all the years
sitting in my room, staring
at the ceiling — thinking —

thanks, Mullumbimby — 7 times
I've visited you — thanks Ocean Shores — and
Lennox Head — where I've never been — except
when we picked up Mia's shoes — and
drove with Luna to Woodburn
to help with the floods —

thank you, Lismore — for the first
water filter in my life — thanks to Emma
for the lift — and the sex afterwards — thanks to
Ballina Service Centre; for the driver's license
I've never gotten —

thanks to Yamba, Kingscliff; all the places
I've heard about — thanks to Federal —
where Thea showed me — for the flirt — and
you know — the Gold Coast — oh, how ugly

you are – Brisbane – for the shitty gig
Vincent took me to for my birthday –

thanks, Byron Bay – for your
superficial people – superficial –
but beautiful and pure, kind – so
kind – thanks
for the mature ways
you approach – and heal – my
judgemental attitude –

thank you, Byron Bay – for showing me
there's beauty – you can trust – for
the peace
I never felt before – the acceptance
not even cultured Europe
could offer –

I appreciate you, Cavanbah, your nature
and your people – I appreciate
the truth of you
hidden
underneath those who destroy you – I love you
Cavanbah:
sweet land of thee
the land
of liberty – and am
forever
in respect

1 minute silence

on Anzac day
3 years ago
I was living
at a dog shelter –

the owner, she
woke me up
in the morning, took
two
plastic chairs

and put them on the main road
where we sat down –

"my father," she said, "he left
through here –"

I was
two continents away
from home – living
in a caravan, taking care
of dogs –

and I, too, knew how it felt
to watch my father disappear –

the other day I heard
she died; another messenger
of first-hand events
left to see
how do we do it ourselves:

to protect freedom –

I didn't speak
much English
back then

but

I think I understood
the tears
in her eyes — the reflection of her parents
in her
tears —

and the 1 minute
silence
when we stood up —

for the dead

happy for now

so I just finished my shift
and had the best dinner
of
my life — I washed it down
with a fantastically
refrigerated
coca-cola —

even the song I put on
was about to blow up from ecstasy —
after many years — somehow —
I felt
happy —

I had a look at that happy face of mine
in the mirror
over the bar —
what a fucking face
I thought
what a privileged fucking face
a face
with no scars —

then this face suddenly morphed
into different ones — I saw
these
disfigured faces
powerless faces
these hungry faces — begging
for help — women and men
being tortured — eyes
gouged out — skulls smashed —

they disappeared
into the next sip
of that delicious coke –

I went to sit out
on the terrace
to extend my happiness
with a cigarette:

oh my
god, man – *what
a life*, I thought – *what a
beautiful
life* – 2 am – empty streets –
you could hear the ocean
50 m from you – I felt
happy
like never before –

there was a war in Europe – and
here? – the land
was stolen –
everything seemed
okay
here – I turned off
the dishwasher – locked
the restaurant – and
went
home –

happy
for now

here it comes again

here we go again
my dear
they're after me
again
handing me all these pills
and all kinds of drinks —
you know I am
happily into it, and
the sad
tomorrows —

they're jumping all around
talking shallow things again —
I'm guzzling it all
again
and in a few hours
I'm begging for more
when complimenting on their lives
that seem to me evil and sad
when I'm sober —

here it is again —
waking up, tearing my hair out
not remembering
last night
in this strange town
with all these strange people —

I can't keep my feet on the ground
my dear —
the pills have betrayed
all the muscular bullshit I said —

all the strength has disappeared
in a stupid, selfish
uneducated softness –

and you're not around anymore –
a new day has begun
and I didn't refuse what I stand against
again
what you seemed to like about me
I've lost
again
your confidence, I've broken
again –

here it comes
again

to the sun

Milton Keynes UK
Ingram Content Group UK Ltd.
UKHW021115030424
440506UK00006B/670

9 780646 892917